Saving Antarctica

by Meish Goldish

SCHOOL PUBLISHERS

Printed in China

ISBN 10: 0-15-350311-4
ISBN 13: 978-0-15-350311-5

Ordering Options
ISBN 10: 0-15-349941-9 (Grade 6 ELL Collection)
ISBN 13: 978-0-15-349941-8 (Grade 6 ELL Collection)
ISBN 10: 0-15-357355-4 (package of 5)
ISBN 13: 978-0-15-357355-2 (package of 5)

5 6 7 8 9 10   0940   12 11 10 09

Antarctica is the coldest land on earth. Antarctica is mostly covered with snow and ice. Few kinds of animals can live there.

You might think no one travels to Antarctica. That is not true. Many people go there. Scientists work there to find more about Antarctica. People travel there to see the land and animals.

The land and animals of Antarctica are in danger. Now countries are working together to protect the environment. They want to protect Antarctica. They want to keep the land safe.

Sled Dogs

For years, people in Antarctica traveled by dogsled. They used sled dogs such as huskies to pull the sleds. Dogs like huskies are strong animals. The huskies did a good job. However, they caused some problems, too. Their barking and running scared other animals.

Today people in Antarctica don't use huskies. People use motor sleds instead. These have their own set of environmental problems. Noise and pollution are two of the biggest ones.

Seals

Many seals live in Antarctica. One kind is the fur seal. Another kind is the southern elephant seal. People have hunted both kinds.

Years ago, hunters killed millions of seals. People hunted fur seals for their fur. They hunted southern elephant seals for their body oil. The fur and oil were used to make various products for people. Nearly the entire seal population in Antarctica was wiped out.

Today there are laws against seal hunting in Antarctica. The seals are now protected.

Whales

Many whales live in the waters of Antarctica. In the past, hunters killed a large number of whales. People used whales for their body fat. The fat was used to make oil. Some kinds of whales almost disappeared completely. They were almost driven to extinction.

New laws were passed. They limited the number of whales that could be hunted. Today, Antarctica is a safer place for whales. No whale hunting is allowed there.

Fish

Ice covers the waters of Antarctica. Fish swim under the ice. There are fish called icefish and toothfish. There are Antarctic cod.

You might think the fish are safe under the ice. After all, who can fish for them there? The answer may surprise you. Large fishing boats cut through the ice. Then large nets are spread to catch the fish in the water.

For years, the fish population in Antarctica dropped. Now laws protect the fish. Fishing is still allowed. However, it is limited.

Krill

The waters of Antarctica are also home to krill. They are tiny sea animals. They look like little shrimp. They travel in large groups.

Krill are very popular in Antarctica. Many animals eat krill. Animals depend on krill for food. Whales eat lots of krill. Seals and penguins eat krill, too. Krill are healthy for them.

People catch krill, too. People sell krill to companies that raise fish. The fish are fed krill. The krill keep the fish healthy. Then the fish are sold for food.

People taking krill from the waters of Antarctica caused a problem. The animals that eat krill didn't have enough to eat. Whales and seals went hungry. Penguins and other birds were hungry, too. The survival of these animals was in danger.

Today there are new laws. They limit the number of krill that people can take. Now other animals have enough krill to eat.

Penguins

Many penguins live in Antarctica. Scientists have studied the penguins for years. Scientists keep track of the penguin population. They want to know whether it goes up or down.

Scientists have come up with a way to keep track of the penguins. Scientists glue a special tag to each penguin's beak. The tags help scientists count the penguins. The tags show their travels. The scientists track each bird by its bar code.

There are fewer penguins in Antarctica now than in the past. Scientists think that this is because the winters are getting warmer. Some penguins spend more time on the ice. Other penguins spend more time in the water. Some of the ice will melt during a warm winter. That leads to more water and less ice for the penguins. The penguins in the water have a bigger home. The penguins on the ice have a smaller home.

The size of a penguin's home is important. A larger home means more food in the area. A smaller home means less food. Less food makes life harder for the penguins. Some do not survive.

Scientists want to help the penguins. Scientists want to know why the winters are turning warmer. Scientists want to know why more ice is melting in Antarctica. They want to keep the environment safe for the birds.

Global Warming

Scientists study the weather in Antarctica. The air has gotten warmer in past years. More ice has melted. That isn't good. Why is the weather in Antarctica getting warmer?

Scientists argue about this. Most believe the answer is "global warming." Layers of gases lie between the earth and the sun. Some of these layers keep warmth inside of the earth's atmosphere. People do things that add to these layers of gas. This keeps more of the warmth from the sun on earth. More ice will melt in Antarctica as the earth becomes warmer.

Antarctica has another environmental problem. The problem is a hole in a layer of gas around the earth called the ozone layer. Ozone protects living things on the earth from the more harmful rays of the sun. These rays can harm people's skin.

Each year, certain human-made chemicals drift high into the air and weaken the ozone layer. The hole that forms may be putting the animals and people of Antarctica in danger.

Many scientists and world leaders want to stop these problems. All over the world, people are already taking action. We are learning that keeping Antarctica safe keeps everyone safe!

Scaffolded Language Development

SUFFIX *-ION* On the board, write the concept words *population, protection, extinction,* and *pollution.* Point out that these words all end with the suffix *-ion.* Explain that when this suffix is added to a verb, the word becomes a noun that means "the act of" or "the state of" doing something. Point out that when a verb ends with *-e,* the final vowel is dropped before adding *-ion.*

Ask students to turn these verbs into nouns by adding the suffix *–ion*:

> *celebrate*
> *circulate*
> *evaporate*
> *immigrate*

Have students use one of the nouns they made above to complete the following sentences:

1. Water is turned into vapor through _____.
2. Many people came to this country in the early 1900s, a period of increased _____.
3. The _____ of blood through your body is controlled by your heart.
4. People like to eat, sing, and dance at a _____.

 ## Science

Penguin Study Have students research baby penguins and how they survive in the cold. Ask students to make a poster of their findings.

School-Home Connection

Weather Report Have students discuss with a friend or family member how the weather affects their life. What do people need to do to keep safe in bad weather?

Word Count: 979